An Encyclopaed and Roman and Heroes

written by Brian Moses

How to use this encyclopaedia

This book will help you to find out about the gods and heroes of mythology. The Greeks and Romans often had the same gods and heroes but gave them different names. In this book they are listed in alphabetical order, with the Greek (Grk) name first. Where gods or heroes are cross-referred, their names appear in colour, followed by a page number. To find out about Roman (Rmn) gods and heroes, look them up in the index at the back of the book.

 LONGMAN

Achilles (Grk hero)

Son of the sea-nymph Thetis, who immersed him in the River Styx when he was a baby. This gave him protection against injury, except at the heel by which she held on to him. During the siege of Troy, Achilles was a brave commander in the Greek army but was killed by a poisoned arrow in his heel.

Thetis and Achilles.

Aeneas (Rmn hero)

Son of Venus (p. 4), goddess of love and a Trojan prince, Anchises. Aeneas escaped from Troy and sailed for Italy but was shipwrecked on the African coast. Dido, the Queen of Carthage, fell in love with him but took her own life when he refused to take her to Italy. Aeneas' destiny was to found the Roman people and his story is told by Vergil in *The Aeneid*.

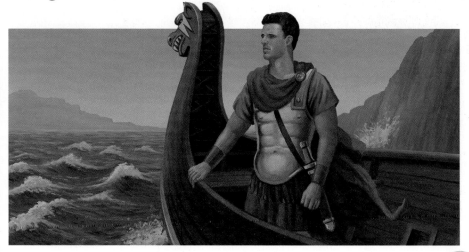

Aphrodite (Grk), Venus (Rmn)

Goddess of love, beauty and fertility. Daughter of the Titan Uranus. She was born fully-grown from the foam that rose up when a drop of his blood fell into the ocean, then carried on a scallop shell to the island of Cyprus (where Aphrodite's Rock is named after her).

The Birth of Venus by Botticelli, c. 1485, Uffizi Gallery, Florence, Italy.

Apollo (Grk), Phoebus (Rmn)

Son of Zeus (p. 23). God of the sun, responsible for the sun's movement across the sky. He was also the god of poetry, music, hunting and prophecy (predicting the future). The Temple at Delphi was the place where priests or priestesses delivered most of his prophecies to the people.

Ares (Grk), Mars (Rmn)

God of war, son of Zeus (p. 23) and Hera (p. 12). Ares was unpopular among the gods on Mount Olympus except for Aphrodite, who fell in love with him. Mars was the father of Romulus (p. 21), the founder of Rome. Also god of fertility, his month March is a time of new growth.

Artemis (Grk), Diana (Rmn)

Goddess of the moon and of hunting, daughter of Zeus (p. 23), twin sister of Apollo (p. 5).

Artemis had a fierce temper: she turned the hunter Actaeon into a stag when he happened to see her bathing. The Temple of Artemis at Ephesus in Turkey was one of the seven wonders of the ancient world.

Athene or Athena (Grk), Minerva (Rmn)

Goddess of power and wisdom. Protector of Greek heroes. Daughter of Zeus (p. 23), born from his forehead, fully-grown and wearing armour. She was her father's favourite child and he gave her his shield which had the emblem of Medusa on it. The city of Athens was named after her.

Dionysus (Grk), Bacchus (Rmn)

God of wine and the theatre. Often pictured on Greek vases with vine branches and a drinking horn. Son of Zeus (p. 23) and a mortal woman Siemele who had been killed by Zeus' lightning. Dionysus was kept safe by being sewn into Zeus' thigh from where he was eventually born.

Eros (Grk), Cupid (Rmn)

God of love. Young, handsome and mischievous. Eros carried a golden bow and arrows. Anyone shot by his arrows immediately fell in love. Eros fell in love himself with the mortal maiden Psyche when he was grazed by one of his own arrows.

Hades or Pluto (Grk), Dis (Rmn)

God of the dead. Brother of Zeus (p. 23) and Poseidon (p. 20). Hades was given the Underworld as his kingdom when the three brothers defeated their father, Cronos. The name Pluto means 'Lord of Riches' as he was believed to hold all the precious metals and jewels below ground.

Hera (Grk), Juno (Rmn)

Goddess of marriage, her chief role was ensuring the well-being of women. She married her brother Zeus (p. 23) and became queen of the gods. She became bitter with Zeus over his love for other women and plotted against him. Zeus punished her by tying anvils to her feet and suspending her in chains.

Heracles or Hercules (Grk hero)

Famed for strength, son of Zeus (p. 23) and a mortal Alceme. Zeus's jealous wife Hera (p. 12) tried to kill Heracles when he was a baby, then drove him insane so that he murdered his wife and children. He was given twelve tasks as a punishment (the labours of Heracles).

Hercules fighting the Nemean lion.

Hermes (Grk), Mercury (Rmn)

Messenger of the gods. Responsible for good luck and wealth. He was a special herald of Zeus (p. 23) who gave him winged sandals and a magic staff. Hermes accompanied the souls of the dead to the Underworld.

Janus (Rmn)

God of doors and beginnings. Represented as having two faces, one looking forward and the other backwards. January, the first month of the year, is named after Janus. His temple had doors facing east and west. These were kept closed in peacetime and opened when Rome went to war.

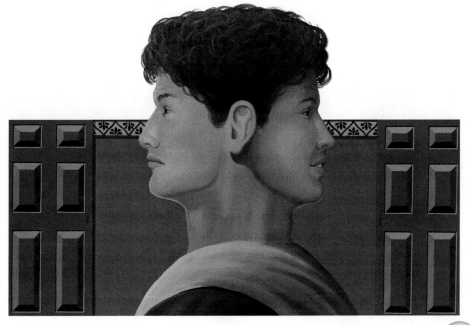

Jason (Grk hero)

Jason sailed on a dangerous voyage with a group of heroic young men, the Argonauts. His object was to bring back the Golden Fleece and regain the kingdom that his uncle Pelias had taken from him. With the aid of a sleeping potion provided by the princess Medea, Jason was able to subdue the fierce dragon that guarded the fleece and return with it to Greece.

Odysseus (Grk) Ulysses (Rmn)

Greek hero who fought bravely at Troy. It is written that he first proposed the idea of the Trojan Horse as a way of conquering Troy. His journey home took ten years during which he was shipwrecked a number of times and encountered monsters such as the one-eyed Cyclops Polyphemus. His adventures are recounted by Homer in *The Odyssey*.

Pan (Grk), Faunus (Rmn)

God of the woods and fields, god of shepherds and their flocks. Son of Hermes (p. 14). Pan's goat horns and hoofs frightened people. He played music on his pipes to enchant woodland nymphs but his ugliness inspired 'panic'.

Perseus (Grk hero)

Killed the gorgon Medusa. The goddess Athene gave him a sharp sword and a shield to protect him from Medusa's gaze, for anyone who looked on her was instantly turned to stone. He was also given winged sandals and a cap of invisibility. With the help of these he was able to cut off Medusa's head and escape with it. Perseus married Andromeda whom he saved from a sea monster.

Poseidon (Grk), Neptune (Rmn)

God of the sea, brother of Zeus (p. 23) and Hades (p. 11). Father of the Cyclops, Polyphemus who imprisoned Odysseus (p. 17) on his travels. Both Poseidon and Neptune are shown as stately, bearded figures, usually holding a trident which was used to stir up storms at sea.

Romulus (Rmn hero)

Romulus and his twin brother Remus were fathered by Mars (p. 6) the god of war and the priestess Rhea Silvia. She threw them into the river Tiber but they were discovered and nursed by a she-wolf. They were then reared by a shepherd and his wife. They decided to build a new city, but Romulus killed Remus in a violent quarrel. The city was Rome, and Romulus became its first ruler.

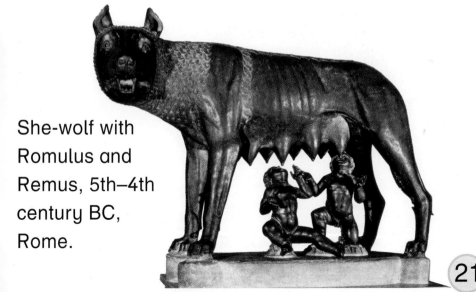

She-wolf with Romulus and Remus, 5th–4th century BC, Rome.

21

Theseus (Grk hero)

Son of Aegeus, king of Athens. Like Heracles (p. 13), whom he admired, Theseus slew many monsters. His most famous exploit was the killing of the Minotaur, a creature half-bull, half-human that inhabited the Labyrinth under the King of Crete's palace. Later on, he tried to rescue Persephone from the Underworld but was imprisoned by Hades (p. 11) and then released by Heracles.

Zeus (Grk), Jupiter (Rmn)

King of the gods on Mount Olympus who fought and dethroned his father, the Titan Cronus. Zeus married his sister Hera (p. 12) and had many children, some with goddesses, some with mortals. Zeus sent thunderbolts to punish his enemies. A 12-metre statue of Zeus at Olympia made of gold, marble and ivory was one of the seven wonders of the ancient world.

Index